Gareth Stevens
PUBLISHING

T0004812

My Day at School

Getting Ready for School

by Joanne Mattern

Reading consultant: Susan Nations, M.Ed.,
author/literacy coach/
consultant in literacy development

Please visit our web site at: www.garethstevens.com
For a free color catalog describing our list of high-quality books,
call 1-800-542-2595 (USA) or 1-800-387-3178 (Canada).
Our fax: 877-542-2596

Library of Congress Cataloging-in-Publication Data

Mattern, Joanne, 1963-
    Getting ready for school / by Joanne Mattern.
        p. cm. — (My day at school)
    Includes bibliographical references and index.
    ISBN-10: 0-8368-6785-8 — ISBN-13: 978-0-8368-6785-5 (lib. bdg.)
    ISBN-10: 0-8368-6792-0 — ISBN-13: 978-0-8368-6792-3 (softcover)
    1. School childen—Juvenile literature. 2. Morning customs—Juvenile literature. I. Title.
  HQ781.M364   2006
  372.18—dc22   2006005137

Copyright © 2007 by Gareth Stevens Inc.

Editor: Barbara Kiely Miller
Art direction: Tammy West
Cover design and page layout: Kami Strunsee
Picture research: Diane Laska-Swanke
Photographer: Gregg Andersen

Printed in the United States of America

1 2 3 4 5 6 7 8 9 10 09 08 07 06

Note to Educators and Parents

Reading is such an exciting adventure for young children! They are beginning to integrate their oral language skills with written language. To encourage children along the path to early literacy, books must be colorful, engaging, and interesting; they should invite the young reader to explore both the print and the pictures.

The *My Day at School* series is designed to help young readers review the routines and rules of a school day, while learning new vocabulary and strengthening their reading comprehension. In simple, easy-to-read language, each book follows a child through part of a typical school day.

Each book is specially designed to support the young reader in the reading process. The familiar topics are appealing to young children and invite them to read — and re-read — again and again. The full-color photographs and enhanced text further support the student during the reading process.

In addition to serving as wonderful picture books in schools, libraries, homes, and other places where children learn to love reading, these books are specifically intended to be read within an instructional guided reading group. This small group setting allows beginning readers to work with a fluent adult model as they make meaning from the text. After children develop fluency with the text and content, the book can be read independently. Children and adults alike will find these books supportive, engaging, and fun!

— Susan Nations, M.Ed., author, literacy coach,
and consultant in literacy development

Mom wakes me up early. It is time to get ready for school.

First, I wash my face and hands. The warm water and the **bubbles** in the soap make me feel clean.

Next, I get dressed. I will wear my purple shirt today. Purple is my favorite color.

Mom brushes my hair. She makes a ponytail for me.

Now it is time for **breakfast**.
Cereal and milk are my
favorites.

Dad helps me learn my spelling words. I spell the words for Dad.

I brush my teeth after breakfast.   I also wash my hands again.

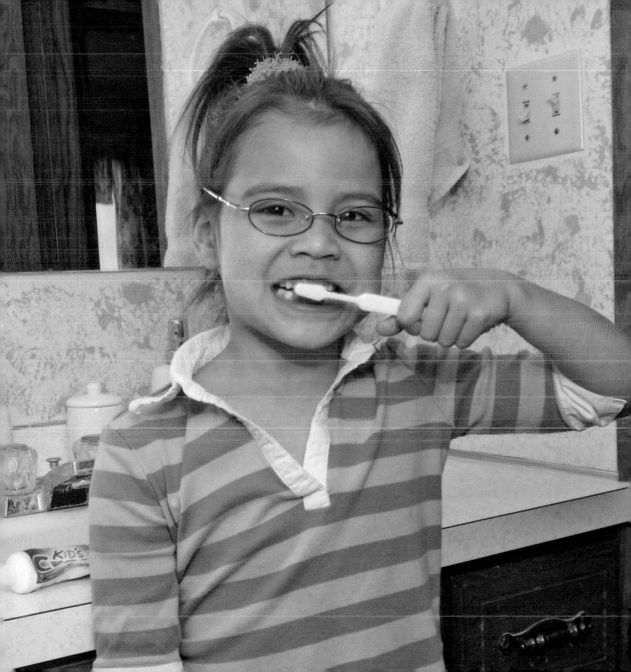

I have all my books and pencils. I have my **lunchbox**, too.

I am ready for school. I know
I will have a good day!

Glossary

breakfast — the first meal of the day

bubbles — balls of air with a thin covering, such as soap, around each one

cereal — a breakfast food made from grains

favorite — something or someone that is liked more than all others

lunchbox — a box with a handle, used to carry food

For More Information

Books

Bread and Cereal. Let's Read About Food (series). Cynthia Klingel and Robert B. Noyed (Gareth Stevens)

Brushing Well. Dental Health (series). Helen Frost (Capstone)

Harry Gets Ready for School. Harriet Ziefert (Puffin)

Web Site

Smile Kids — Brushing and Flossing
smilekids.deltadentalca.org/brushing.html
Tips on brushing and flossing teeth; games and interesting facts about teeth

Index

books 18
breakfast 12, 16
brushing hair 10

brushing teeth 16
cereal 12
dressing 8
lunchboxes 18

milk 12
pencils 18
spelling 14
waking up 4
washing 6, 16

About the Author

Joanne Mattern has written more than one hundred and fifty books for children. Joanne also works in her local library. She lives in New York State with her husband, three daughters, and assorted pets. She enjoys animals, music, going to baseball games, reading, and visiting schools to talk about her books.